MY UNICORN
AUTHORS

DESIGNED BY
TEECEE DESIGN STUDIO

AUTHOR: _______________________________

TITLE	SERIES NAME	BOOK NUMBER	KINDLE/PAPERBACK	RELEASE DATE

NOTES

____

____

____

____

AUTHOR: _______________________

Title	Series Name	Book Number	Kindle/Paperback	Release Date

Notes

____

____

____

____

AUTHOR: _______________________________

Title	Series Name	Book Number	Kindle/Paperback	Release Date

NOTES

____

____

____

____

AUTHOR: ________________________

Title	Series Name	Book Number	Kindle/Paperback	Release Date

NOTES

____

____

____

____

AUTHOR: ______________________________

TITLE	SERIES NAME	BOOK NUMBER	KINDLE/PAPERBACK	RELEASE DATE

NOTES

____

____

____

____

AUTHOR: _______________________________

Title	Series Name	Book Number	Kindle/Paperback	Release Date

NOTES

____

____

____

____

AUTHOR: _______________________________

Title	Series Name	Book Number	Kindle/Paperback	Release Date

NOTES

____

____

____

____

Author: ________________________

Title	Series Name	Book Number	Kindle/Paperback	Release Date

Notes

____

____

____

____

AUTHOR: ______________________________

TITLE	SERIES NAME	BOOK NUMBER	KINDLE/PAPERBACK	RELEASE DATE

NOTES

____

____

____

____

AUTHOR: _______________________________

TITLE	SERIES NAME	BOOK NUMBER	KINDLE/PAPERBACK	RELEASE DATE

NOTES

____

____

____

____

AUTHOR: _______________________________

Title	Series Name	Book Number	Kindle/Paperback	Release Date

NOTES

____

____

____

____

AUTHOR: _______________________________

TITLE	SERIES NAME	BOOK NUMBER	KINDLE/PAPERBACK	RELEASE DATE

NOTES

____

____

____

____

AUTHOR: _______________________________

Title	Series Name	Book Number	Kindle/Paperback	Release Date

NOTES

____

____

____

____

AUTHOR: ________________________________

Title	Series Name	Book Number	Kindle/Paperback	Release Date

NOTES

____

____

____

____

AUTHOR: ___________________________

TITLE	SERIES NAME	BOOK NUMBER	KINDLE/PAPERBACK	RELEASE DATE

NOTES

____

____

____

____

AUTHOR: _______________________________

TITLE	SERIES NAME	BOOK NUMBER	KINDLE/PAPERBACK	RELEASE DATE

NOTES

____

____

____

____

AUTHOR: ________________________________

TITLE	SERIES NAME	BOOK NUMBER	KINDLE/PAPERBACK	RELEASE DATE

NOTES

____

____

____

____

AUTHOR: _______________________________

TITLE	SERIES NAME	BOOK NUMBER	KINDLE/PAPERBACK	RELEASE DATE

NOTES

____

____

____

____

AUTHOR: _______________________________

TITLE	SERIES NAME	BOOK NUMBER	KINDLE/PAPERBACK	RELEASE DATE

NOTES

____

____

____

____

AUTHOR: _______________________________

Title	Series Name	Book Number	Kindle/Paperback	Release Date

NOTES

____

____

____

____

AUTHOR: _______________________________

Title	Series Name	Book Number	Kindle/Paperback	Release Date

NOTES

____

____

____

____

AUTHOR: ________________________________

TITLE	SERIES NAME	BOOK NUMBER	KINDLE/PAPERBACK	RELEASE DATE

NOTES

____

____

____

____

AUTHOR: _________________________

TITLE	SERIES NAME	BOOK NUMBER	KINDLE/PAPERBACK	RELEASE DATE

NOTES

____

____

____

____

AUTHOR: _______________________________

TITLE	SERIES NAME	BOOK NUMBER	KINDLE/PAPERBACK	RELEASE DATE

NOTES

____

____

____

____

AUTHOR: _______________________________

TITLE	SERIES NAME	BOOK NUMBER	KINDLE/PAPERBACK	RELEASE DATE

NOTES

____

____

____

____

AUTHOR: _______________________

Title	Series Name	Book Number	Kindle/Paperback	Release Date

NOTES

____

____

____

____

Author: ______________________

Title	Series Name	Book Number	Kindle/Paperback	Release Date

Notes

____

____

____

____

AUTHOR: _______________________________

TITLE	SERIES NAME	BOOK NUMBER	KINDLE/PAPERBACK	RELEASE DATE

NOTES

____

____

____

____

AUTHOR: ______________________________

Title	Series Name	Book Number	Kindle/Paperback	Release Date

NOTES

____

____

____

____

AUTHOR: _______________________________

TITLE	SERIES NAME	BOOK NUMBER	KINDLE/PAPERBACK	RELEASE DATE

NOTES

____

____

____

____

AUTHOR: _______________________________

Title	Series Name	Book Number	Kindle/Paperback	Release Date

NOTES

____

____

____

____

AUTHOR: ______________________________

Title	Series Name	Book Number	Kindle/Paperback	Release Date

Notes

____

____

____

____

AUTHOR: _______________________

Title	Series Name	Book Number	Kindle/Paperback	Release Date

NOTES

____

____

____

____

TITLE	SERIES NAME	BOOK NUMBER	KINDLE/PAPERBACK	RELEASE DATE

NOTES

____

____

____

____

AUTHOR: _______________________________

TITLE	SERIES NAME	BOOK NUMBER	KINDLE/PAPERBACK	RELEASE DATE

NOTES

____

____

____

____

AUTHOR: _______________________________

Title	Series Name	Book Number	Kindle/Paperback	Release Date

NOTES

____

____

____

____

AUTHOR: _______________________________

Title	Series Name	Book Number	Kindle/Paperback	Release Date

NOTES

____

____

____

____

Author: _______________________________

Title	Series Name	Book Number	Kindle/Paperback	Release Date

Notes

____

____

____

____

AUTHOR: _______________________

Title	Series Name	Book Number	Kindle/Paperback	Release Date

NOTES

____

____

____

____

AUTHOR: _______________________________

TITLE	SERIES NAME	BOOK NUMBER	KINDLE/PAPERBACK	RELEASE DATE

NOTES

____

____

____

____

AUTHOR: _______________________________

Title	Series Name	Book Number	Kindle/Paperback	Release Date

Notes

____

____

____

____

AUTHOR: _______________________________

TITLE	SERIES NAME	BOOK NUMBER	KINDLE/PAPERBACK	RELEASE DATE

NOTES

____

____

____

____

AUTHOR: ________________________

Title	Series Name	Book Number	Kindle/Paperback	Release Date

NOTES

____

____

____

____

Title	Series Name	Book Number	Kindle/Paperback	Release Date

NOTES

Title	Series Name	Book Number	Kindle/Paperback	Release Date

NOTES
____
____
____
____

Author: ________________________________

Title	Series Name	Book Number	Kindle/Paperback	Release Date

Notes

____

____

____

____

AUTHOR: ______________________________

Title	Series Name	Book Number	Kindle/Paperback	Release Date

NOTES

____

____

____

____

Author: ___________________________________

Title	Series Name	Book Number	Kindle/Paperback	Release Date

Notes

____

____

____

____

AUTHOR: _______________________________

Title	Series Name	Book Number	Kindle/Paperback	Release Date

NOTES

____

____

____

____

AUTHOR: _______________________________

Title	Series Name	Book Number	Kindle/Paperback	Release Date

NOTES

____

____

____

____

Author: ___________________________________

Title	Series Name	Book Number	Kindle/Paperback	Release Date

Notes

____

____

____

____

Title	Series Name	Book Number	Kindle/Paperback	Release Date

NOTES

____

____

____

____

AUTHOR: _______________________________

TITLE	SERIES NAME	BOOK NUMBER	KINDLE/PAPERBACK	RELEASE DATE

NOTES

____

____

____

____

AUTHOR: _______________________________

TITLE	SERIES NAME	BOOK NUMBER	KINDLE/PAPERBACK	RELEASE DATE

NOTES

____

____

____

____

AUTHOR: ___________________________

TITLE	SERIES NAME	BOOK NUMBER	KINDLE/PAPERBACK	RELEASE DATE

NOTES

____

____

____

____

TITLE	SERIES NAME	BOOK NUMBER	KINDLE/PAPERBACK	RELEASE DATE

NOTES

____

____

____

____

AUTHOR: ________________________________

Title	Series Name	Book Number	Kindle/Paperback	Release Date

Notes

____

____

____

____

AUTHOR: _______________________________

TITLE	SERIES NAME	BOOK NUMBER	KINDLE/PAPERBACK	RELEASE DATE

NOTES

____

____

____

____

AUTHOR: _______________________________

Title	Series Name	Book Number	Kindle/Paperback	Release Date

NOTES

____

____

____

____

AUTHOR: _______________________________

Title	Series Name	Book Number	Kindle/Paperback	Release Date

NOTES

____

____

____

____

Author: ________________________________

Title	Series Name	Book Number	Kindle/Paperback	Release Date

Notes

____

____

____

____

AUTHOR: ________________________________

TITLE	SERIES NAME	BOOK NUMBER	KINDLE/PAPERBACK	RELEASE DATE

NOTES

____

____

____

____

AUTHOR: _______________________________

Title	Series Name	Book Number	Kindle/Paperback	Release Date

NOTES

____

____

____

____

AUTHOR: ______________________________

Title	Series Name	Book Number	Kindle/Paperback	Release Date

NOTES

____

____

____

____

AUTHOR: ___________________________

TITLE	SERIES NAME	BOOK NUMBER	KINDLE/PAPERBACK	RELEASE DATE

NOTES

____

____

____

____

AUTHOR: _______________________________

Title	Series Name	Book Number	Kindle/Paperback	Release Date

NOTES
____

____

____

____

AUTHOR: ______________________________

Title	Series Name	Book Number	Kindle/Paperback	Release Date

NOTES

____

____

____

____

AUTHOR: _______________________

Title	Series Name	Book Number	Kindle/Paperback	Release Date

NOTES

____

____

____

____

AUTHOR: _______________________________

TITLE	SERIES NAME	BOOK NUMBER	KINDLE/PAPERBACK	RELEASE DATE

NOTES

____

____

____

____

AUTHOR: ________________________________

Title	Series Name	Book Number	Kindle/Paperback	Release Date

NOTES

____

____

____

____

AUTHOR: ______________________________

Title	Series Name	Book Number	Kindle/Paperback	Release Date

NOTES

____

____

____

____

AUTHOR: _______________________________

Title	Series Name	Book Number	Kindle/Paperback	Release Date

NOTES

____

____

____

____

Title	Series Name	Book Number	Kindle/Paperback	Release Date

NOTES

____

____

____

____

AUTHOR: _______________________________

TITLE	SERIES NAME	BOOK NUMBER	KINDLE/PAPERBACK	RELEASE DATE

NOTES

____

____

____

____

AUTHOR: ________________________

TITLE	SERIES NAME	BOOK NUMBER	KINDLE/PAPERBACK	RELEASE DATE

NOTES

____

____

____

____

AUTHOR: _______________________________

TITLE	SERIES NAME	BOOK NUMBER	KINDLE/PAPERBACK	RELEASE DATE

NOTES

____

____

____

____

AUTHOR: _______________________________

TITLE	SERIES NAME	BOOK NUMBER	KINDLE/PAPERBACK	RELEASE DATE

NOTES

____

____

____

____

AUTHOR: ______________________

TITLE	SERIES NAME	BOOK NUMBER	KINDLE/PAPERBACK	RELEASE DATE

NOTES

____

____

____

____

AUTHOR: _______________________________

TITLE	SERIES NAME	BOOK NUMBER	KINDLE/PAPERBACK	RELEASE DATE

NOTES

____

____

____

____

Title	Series Name	Book Number	Kindle/Paperback	Release Date

Notes

____

____

____

____

Title	Series Name	Book Number	Kindle/Paperback	Release Date

NOTES

____

____

____

____

TITLE	SERIES NAME	BOOK NUMBER	KINDLE/PAPERBACK	RELEASE DATE

NOTES

____

____

____

____

AUTHOR: _______________________________

Title	Series Name	Book Number	Kindle/Paperback	Release Date

NOTES

____

____

____

____

AUTHOR: ___________________________

Title	Series Name	Book Number	Kindle/Paperback	Release Date

NOTES

____

____

____

____

Title	Series Name	Book Number	Kindle/Paperback	Release Date

NOTES

AUTHOR: ________________________________

Title	Series Name	Book Number	Kindle/Paperback	Release Date

NOTES

AUTHOR: _______________________________

Title	Series Name	Book Number	Kindle/Paperback	Release Date

NOTES

____

____

____

____

AUTHOR: ______________________________

TITLE	SERIES NAME	BOOK NUMBER	KINDLE/PAPERBACK	RELEASE DATE

NOTES

____

____

____

____

Author: _______________________________

Title	Series Name	Book Number	Kindle/Paperback	Release Date

Notes

____

____

____

____

AUTHOR: ___________________________

Title	Series Name	Book Number	Kindle/Paperback	Release Date

NOTES

____

____

____

____

AUTHOR: __________________________

TITLE	SERIES NAME	BOOK NUMBER	KINDLE/PAPERBACK	RELEASE DATE

NOTES

____

____

____

____

AUTHOR: _______________________________

Title	Series Name	Book Number	Kindle/Paperback	Release Date

NOTES

____

____

____

____

Author: _______________________________

Title	Series Name	Book Number	Kindle/Paperback	Release Date

Notes

____

____

____

____

AUTHOR: _______________________________

TITLE	SERIES NAME	BOOK NUMBER	KINDLE/PAPERBACK	RELEASE DATE

NOTES

____

____

____

____

TITLE	SERIES NAME	BOOK NUMBER	KINDLE/PAPERBACK	RELEASE DATE

NOTES

____

____

____

____

AUTHOR: _______________________________

TITLE	SERIES NAME	BOOK NUMBER	KINDLE/PAPERBACK	RELEASE DATE

NOTES

____

____

____

____

AUTHOR: _______________________________

TITLE	SERIES NAME	BOOK NUMBER	KINDLE/PAPERBACK	RELEASE DATE

NOTES

____

____

____

____

Author: _______________________________

Title	Series Name	Book Number	Kindle/Paperback	Release Date

Notes

____

____

____

____

Author: _______________________________

Title	Series Name	Book Number	Kindle/Paperback	Release Date

Notes

____

____

____

____

Thank you so much for your purchase.

I really do hope that this book has helped you,
even in some small way.

Would you like to see different designs/styles?

I am always very happy to hear from customers,
so please feel free to email me on

teeceedesignstudio@yahoo.com